Organic Gardening For Beginners:

Essential Tips on How to Plant and Build an Organic Garden

By

Erin Morrow

Table of Contents

3

Organic Gardening For Beginners: Essential Tips on
How to Plant and Build an Organic Garden

By Erin Morrow

© Copyright 2015 Erin Morrow

This publication is designed to provide accurate and
authoritative information in regard to the subject
matter covered. This work is sold with the
understanding that the publisher is not engaged in
rendering legal, accounting, or other professional
services. If legal advice or other expert assistance is
required, the services of a competent professional
person should be sought.

First Published, 2015

Printed in the United States of America

Introduction

Many people fantasize about having an organic garden in their backyard. Organic means that it is without the use of any chemicals. Of course everyone will enjoy eating and cooking nutritious vegetables. However, before you can start to enjoy those lush green vegetables, you must have a plan to reap the benefits. There are many factors that contribute to making your garden a successful and beautiful one. There are also some challenges you may encounter along the way.

If you have never planted any type of garden before and this is your first time considering an organic garden you will want to develop a comprehensive planting plan. You will need to assess the size of the garden, type of soil you will need, tools you will be using, and amount of water for your garden. Additionally, you will need some expert advice or advice from others who have been successful with gardening. Do not forget that you will need to have a lots of patience and be willing to get your hands dirty. Gardening is not complicated, but it is not easy either, especially if this is your first time. In this book you will find valuable information that will be of great assistance to you, your family and friends. You will learn some tips and tricks for growing the most magnificent organic garden you could ever imagine.

Chapter 1. Benefits of Organic Gardening

Organic Gardens are a great way to eat healthier. Eating organic foods can decrease your family's consumption of pesticides and help to protect the environment from chemicals. Buying organic foods in the store can be more expensive, that is why a garden is a great way to eat organic on a budget.

If you aren't sure where to start, it doesn't take much, start small. Just one or two plants can get you started. Or if you want, you can hire someone to help create your Organic Garden. The benefits of an organic garden affect both you and the world you live in. You will be working toward the greater good of the environment and creating a better, greener and more sound world.

The following are a number of direct benefits that you can gain from an organic gardening experience.

Eating Health Food: This is the primary benefit of organic gardening. Supermarket produce cannot come close to matching the taste or nutrition of a garden vegetable. When you eat directly from your garden you are ensured to consume the highest quality vegetables. There is also no residue of pesticides. Simply put Organic Gardening offers you the most nutritious, cleanest and tastiest fruits and vegetables available.

Knowing What You're Eating: One of the benefits of growing food yourself is that you know exactly where it came from. You also know what it took to get that fruit or vegetable from a seed to an edible product. This increases your satisfaction in the end product.

Saving Money: In most states it is possible to grow vegetables at least six months during the year. Growing your own fruits and vegetables is clearly a money saving practice. You should be able to save about $800 each growing season simply growing your own vegetables. Plus, the supplies needed for gardening are relatively inexpensive.

Being Outdoors: Gardening gets you outdoors. Americans work a lot and due to this we spend about 90 percent of our time inside. A great benefit to gardening is that it gets you outside. This helps to improve your mental and physical health. Being outside also increases your exposure to sunlight. Your plants need sunlight just as much as you. Sunlight provides Vitamin D, which is very important for the maintenance of your bones. It has also been proven that garden soil can help you build a healthy immune system.

Exercise: Exercise is another benefit of organic gardening. Using hand tools in the garden can burn around 200 to 400 calories every hour. If you were to actively garden for six months you can burn about 35,000 calories (which could help you lose up to ten pounds). It is also a great workout for building leg and arm muscles.

Reducing Exposure to Chemicals: Organic Gardening is without Chemicals. This is important because chemicals carry danger and being exposed to pesticides can be linked to a number of different health problems. These health problems include: neurological disorders, reproductive disorders, behavior Issues in children, cancers, weakened immune systems, asthma, Parkinson's disease and many more. Threats of these disorders are eliminated with organic gardening.

Building Knowledge: Another advantage to Organic Gardening is learning. While you learn to imitate the natural environmental system you will learn more and more each year. The more experience you have the more knowledge you can share.

Lifting your Spirits: Gardening is a peaceful hobby. It has proven to have therapeutic benefits on the body. In fact, Horticultural Therapy has been recognized as a treatment in many wellness programs. It is practiced throughout the country and the world.

Promotes Biodiversity: It is important to plant and grow certified organic seeds. Many of these seeds are heirloom. These are important because they offer diversity in food. When you grow an organic garden you are helping to promote and increase this effort.

Discover a New Way of Life: Organic gardening can lead you to a new philosophy of life. Perhaps you will start making other choices that encourage sustainability and ecology. Maybe you will start recycling more and look for alternatives for heat, fuel and light. It can be the start to a new way of life.

Chapter 2. Tips For Starting Your Organic Garden

The following are some great tips you can follow when starting out with your new organic garden.

Make Measurements and Construct Plant Beds – Before you start scattering or planting your seeds, take measurements of the area in which you will be planting. Construct a frame or a number of frames that you will be using for your plant-beds. Three weeks prior to planting, ensure that the ground is dry so when you are tilling or loosening the ground with a pitch fork and a hoe you don't find any hard lumps of soil. When preparing the soil go as deep as 12 inches into the earth and include a layer of half-inch humus. Rake over the surface of the ground and get rid of any small pieces of rocks, weeds or hard lumps of soil. After having cultivated the soil and making your plant beds, keep removing any weeds that might be sprouting and let the soil remain, allowing any other weeds that were hidden beneath the soil to come out.

Shovel a Trench – If you are the type who likes everything to be balanced you can dig out a shallow drain with a hoe. Start your planting in whichever manner you would like. You can plant in rows or grids, whichever form you prefer best and dig shallow holes about less than half inch deep for your seeds or even plant the seeds in small containers.

Planting the Seeds – Place 2 or 3 seeds inside the holes and gently cover them with a little soil. Another option is to follow the instructions on the package the seeds come in. Remember to allow the seeds some space as planting them too close to each other may thin them out.

Cover Seeds with the Soil – As a principle of gardening, simply cover the seeds slightly to avoid stifling them but make sure that they have contact with the soil. This will enable them to germinate properly. Gently cover the seeds with the soil.

Slightly Water Your Planted Seeds – Within the first week of having planted the seeds only mildly water them keeping the soil slightly wet. Don't drench the soil in water as the seeds could be washed away. Soaking the seeds too much is not good for them as they can easily decay. Make sure the surface of the plant beds are moist enough for the seeds to grow and as they start growing, check them daily. As soon as the ground feels dry water the seeds. An important note is that it is always ideal to water the seeds first thing early in the morning and check up on them later in the evening time. You can water the seeds in the late evening after the soil temperature has cooled down. Watering the seeds when the ground is hot could scorch the seeds and damage them.

Following these tips will help you to start a productive garden. An essential key for success is to gently add humus as the weeks go by, to enhance the structure of the soil and add nutrients to boost the microorganisms within the soil. This will foster the development of the seeds.

Basic Gardening Tools

The following are some tools you will need to have when you are starting your garden.

Hand Trowel

Shovel

Pitch Fork

Hoe

Rake

Garden Gloves

Pruning Shears

Wheelbarrow

Sprayer

Leaf Rake

Rubber Boots

What is Transplanting?

Transplant is moving a plant from one location to another. For example, from a pot into the ground. The following is a step by step process for transplanting items into your garden.

Step 1. Dig a hole – You want a hole that is as deep and round as the container the plants were in. Depending on the size of the plant dig a hole that would be ideal to support the plants.

Step 2. Water the plants – Before transplanting water the plants that way the roots get soaked up; this process is allows them to drink water before they are transferred into another area. Secondly, the soil is softened so this way you avoid ripping off any roots during the process of transfer. Maintaining all of the plants roots is vital for growing and rooting into the fresh ground. The more roots a plant has the more nutrients it is capable of absorbing as it develops into a mature plant.

Step 3. Gently transfer the plant from the container – With one hand on top of the container place your fingers around the stem of the plant. Then flip the container upside down and tenderly press or squeeze the plant until it comes out. Do your best to keeping the stem safe from breakage or other damage. If the stem breaks the plants chances of surviving have diminished.

Step 4. Examine the roots – As you inspect the plants it always good to examine the roots. Look to see if the roots have wrapped around the plant. Slowly and gently loosen any roots that may have wrapped around the plant.

Step 5. Plant the plants in the holes – When you place the plant into the hole make sure that the holes are as deep as the containers they were in before. Tomatoes may differ slightly on this as they often require to be planted in deeper holes.

Step 6. Fill up with soil and water plants – After placing the plant in the hole lightly fill up the hole with the soil you had previously removed while digging the holes. Make sure that the roots of the plant have firm contact with the soil. Maintain regular moisture within the soil, as the plants grows bigger and taller the watering process will change.

To ensure success when transplanting do it on a day when it is not too sunny. Granting the plants this privilege allows them to adapt to the weather change and change of environment more successfully.

Chapter 3. How to Maintain Control of The Weeds

Weeds can destroy your plants and can make your garden look neglected. They suck out the water that you pour over your plants and they steal all the nutrients away from the soil within your garden. Since you are growing an organic garden there is no need for the use of chemicals or herbicides. These are toxic to vegetation, wildlife, pets and people. To eliminate weeds here are some strategies you can use to maintain a healthy and vegetating garden.

Strategy #1 Mulching – There are two types of mulching and those are: Organic and Inorganic mulching. Organic mulching may include a blend of cut up leaves, grass, straw, and even humus. Wood chips are also a specialty as well as torn bark from fallen trees, pine needles, sawdust, and even paper. Inorganic mulching entails the use of geotextiles (permeable fabrics specifically for landscaping and gardening), certain types of plastic, gravel and even stones.

Both of these kinds of mulching limit the growth of weeds and increases the nourishment levels of the ground that the plants need. Inorganic mulching may not be as effective in nourishing the soil and plants as the organic does.

What is Mulching? – Mulching controls the weeds by covering the soil to avoid light from reaching the weeds, they grow faster with the presence of light. When you cover the soil, you can toss a layer of organic mulch up to 2 inches in depth or more. Organic mulch will consist of dried grass trimmings, torn leaves, and straw. Experts in gardening recommend you do this every spring and restock your garden throughout the season. Another tip to mulching is that you can use pages of old newspaper and grocery bags to place under the mulch you cover the ground with.

There are a couple benefits to mulching. First, mulching is a timesaver for gardeners and the mulch provides nutrients for your soil as it decays which allows your plants to grow healthy and vibrant. Second, mulch also conserves water and keeps your garden cool. Plus, you won't have to water your plants too many times a day.

Strategy #2 Hand Pulling of Weeds – Now this may sound tedious and tiring but it will benefit you and your garden in the long run. What you do is simply pull weeds from your garden every single day or every week. Always have a bundle of straw or grass to cover up the soil to rid the weeds from growing back quickly.

There are benefits to hand pulling. You will get to know your garden much better and you will be able to identify any issue your garden may have. For example, insects that might be infesting your garden or some plants withering from lack of nutrients. Additionally, you are able to have control over the weeds that keep growing on a daily basis.

Strategy #3 Hoeing Weeds – With a hoe in hand, you simply scoop the weeds from under the ground by the roots. To do this you can hold the hoe with the same grip as when holding a broom, this will minimize the risk of back ache.

The benefit to hoeing your weeds is that your ground will be cultivated and your garden will be weed-less.

Strategy #4 Overexposure to Sunlight – With this process you use the assistance of sunlight. If weeds are growing out of control in a section of your garden you simply pull them out and then cover that section with a layer of a plastic sheet. Leave it there for six weeks and watch the heat kill the rest of the weeds. Make sure to keep an eye on your plants to avoid damaging them.

If you lack patience, the weeds will conquer your garden in a matter of days. Patience is a virtue and in order to avoid weeds destroying your garden pull them out, hoe the weeds, and mulch your garden every day. Keeping control of the weeds will help you have a healthy garden with healthy plants.

Weeds normally grow when the ground is humid which is excellent for your plants to grow. So if you experience a lot of rain it is to your advantage to get rid of all the weeds that will be coming out eventually. Your persistence and consistency to keep your garden clean and plants well watered will produce great benefits for you.

Chapter 4. Controlling Unwanted Creatures in Your Garden

Not all the little creatures and insects crawling around in your garden are bad. Some of them can even be beneficial to your plants. Even those insects that eat plants are a part of the garden you are growing. However, sometimes these pests can get out of hand. The best solution is to use organic methods and products to keep a positive balance. Pesticides are harmful to the user, wildlife and will pollute your water. The following are some tips to preventing and unwanted pests in your garden.

Tip #1 – Grow Healthy Plants: Insects are attracted to plants that are weak and unhealthy. Choose plants that will thrive in your environment. They should not be too wet, dry or shaded. Use compost, it's great for plants!

Tip #2 – Don't Segregate: Mix your flower beds. Combine different herbs, flowers and vegetables together. This will prevent pest from targeting a whole crop.

Tip #3 – Invite Predators: The most natural form of pest control is natural selection. Insects are preyed on by birds, toads, lizards and garden snakes. Don't chase them away, let them eat your insects. Maybe even put up a bird bath or feeder to attract them.

Tip #4 – Barriers: There is a woven fabric called Row Cover. It lets air, water and light reach the plants but keeps deer and other pests out. It can be found at your local garden supply store.

Tip #5 – Choose the Right Treatment: If it's too late for prevention methods, choose the right Organic Treatment. Confirm the pest that is infesting your garden and then pick up the right treatment at your garden store.

Tip #6 – Surrender: If you have enough healthy plants, sacrifice your sickly ones and then the natural insect predators will protect the healthy plants.

Each of these tips will help keep your pest problem under control. It is always best if you can start early and take preventative measures. One great key to success is to look underneath your leaves when applying organic pest control. Insects like to hide under the leaves.

Chapter 5. The Best Plant Combinations For a Healthy Garden

In this section we will discuss great pairings for a healthy garden. If you pair these flowers and herbs you will end up with better soil, increased propagation and your insect problem will be under control. The best part is, there is no need for chemicals.

Combination #1 – Plant Garlic with roses, cucumbers, peas, celery, lettuce and raspberries. Garlic keeps beetles and spiders away from your plants, as well it keeps aphids off roses.

Combination #2 – Plant Sweet Alyssum with broccoli, beans, corn, potatoes and eggplant. The sweet smell attracts predators like wasps to take care of any aphids.

Combination #3 – Plant Borage with strawberries, squash, tomatoes and cucumbers. This will prevent tomato worms and add minerals to the soil.

Combination #4 – Plant Mint with cabbage and tomatoes. Mint grows quickly and keeps away fleas, ants, moths and rodents. Plus, it is a magnet for earthworms and they help improve the soil condition.

Combination #5 – Plant Alfalfa with beans and lettuce. This will add minerals (iron, magnesium, phosphorous and nitrogen) into your soil all year round.

Combination #6 – Plant Scented Marigold with everything. It drives away nematodes and can keep whiteflies away from tomatoes.

Combination #7 – Lavender can be planted with roses, fruit trees and alliums. This will keep fleas and moths away but attract predators like bees, praying mantises and lady bugs.

Combination #8 – Plant Nasturtium with cabbage, radishes, fruit trees and cucumber. This plan keeps away squash bugs, cucumber beetles and whiteflies. It also keeps aphids away from fruit trees.

With these eight great combinations you will have a naturally productive and mutually beneficial organic garden.

Chapter 6. Watering Your Organic Garden

People need to be well hydrated on a hot day. The same is true with any type of garden. It is important to be sure that your plants are well hydrated. Follow these plant watering guidelines for a healthy and vibrant garden.

Choose your Plants Wisely – Plant choice is very important to the success of your garden. You want to be sure that you choose plants that are well suited for the climate, soil and location. If you group your plants by watering needs you can provide more efficient irrigation.

Make sure your Plants take Root – Recently planted gardens need extra attention. It is important to check on new plants often, so that they don't die from insufficient water.

Early Morning or Evening – It is much cooler in the early morning and evening times than during mid-day. The cooler the temperature the less evaporation. You will want to water when the temperature is cooler so that your plants can receive as much moisture as possible.

Two Knuckle Test – Before watering your plants, take your index finger and push into the soil about two knuckles deep. Is it damp? If the ground is damp, do not water. Prioritize your watering. For example, seedlings have small fragile roots and need constant watering. Plants on the top of your priority list should include; transplants, new plants, leave trees, perennials and shrubs.

Drip-Irrigation System – The most efficient use of water will come from a soaker hose or a drip-irrigation system. This system will allow you to select where the water goes.

Say "No" to Weeds and "Yes" to Mulch – Weeds are no good for your garden because they will steal water from your plants. Mulch is great because it can help keep your soil damp by hiding it from the sun.

These are some great guidelines to consider when watering your garden. Ultimately the best key to success, is to make sure your plants receive an inch of water every week. The water can be from a hose or from the rain water.

Chapter 7. Keywords Every Beginning Gardener Should Know

If you are new to organic gardening or gardening in general you will want to be familiar with a few terms. Let's call it your "Garden Vocabulary." This will help you when you are looking for advice from farmers, purchasing supplies at your local gardening store or if you want to impress your friends with your knowledge of Organic Gardening.

Annual: Any plant whose life cycle lasts one season.

Bolting: If the temperature is too warm, some greens like lettuce will grow a flower stalk and germinate seeds. They are bitter and tough to taste and eat.

Compost: Known as "Black Gold" because it is great for the plants and soil. It helps prevent disease and manage moisture. It is usually made of kitchen scraps, animal feces, and other items.

Deadheading: Ridding your garden of drab and old flowers to allow the water and energy to better produce new growth.

Direct Sowing: Using gardening beds for planting and not pots.

Full Shade: This is an area of your garden that doesn't get a lot of sunlight. Usually less than three hours a day. Not many crops and flowers grow well in this environment.

Full Sun: The opposite of Full Shade. An area of your garden that gets at least six hours of sunlight each day. Most crops need Full Sun during growing season.

Hardiness Zones: This will determine if your perennial plant will survive the winter, based on which state you live in.

Heirloom: A plant that has been saved by farmers for many years.

Hybrid: A plant that is created by cross breading for appealing characteristics like pest-resistance.

N, P & K: These are the chemical symbols for nitrogen, phosphorus and potassium. It is often found on packages of fertilizer because it is needed by plants.

Perennial: These are plants that grow year after year without needing to replant.

Soil pH: This is the measure of the soil's acidity or alkalinity. It is very important to know for the productivity of your plant growth. The best soil pH is between 6.5 and 7.0.

Conclusion

If you are choosing to go organic this means that you are not using any pesticides or fertilizers. Organic gardening involves trying to create a more holistic and natural ecosystem. It also offers the gardener a number of benefits both directly and indirectly. If you follow these guidelines, and tips you are sure to have a successful gardening experience with a number of benefits for your body, home and mind.

I want to personally thank you for reading my book. I hope you found information in this book useful and I would be very grateful if you could leave your honest review about this book. I certainly want to thank you in advance for doing this.

If you have the time, you can check my other books too.